MEN'S HARDWEAR

*Dear Frederica,
Thanks for all
of your support,
We ♡ you!
TPB ♡ ♡*

A Gentlemen's Guide *to* Timeless Fashion

TROY P. BOSTON • STYLIST EXTRAORDINAIRE

Cover and model photos by Phelan Marc - www.phelanmarc.com
Stock image, page 54: iStockphoto.com/pialhovik

ISBN-10: 0-9979635-0-6
ISBN-13: 978-0-9979635-0-2

Also available as an ebook on Amazon.com.

Printed in the United States of America.

MEN'S HARDWEAR

A gentlemen's guide to timeless fashion

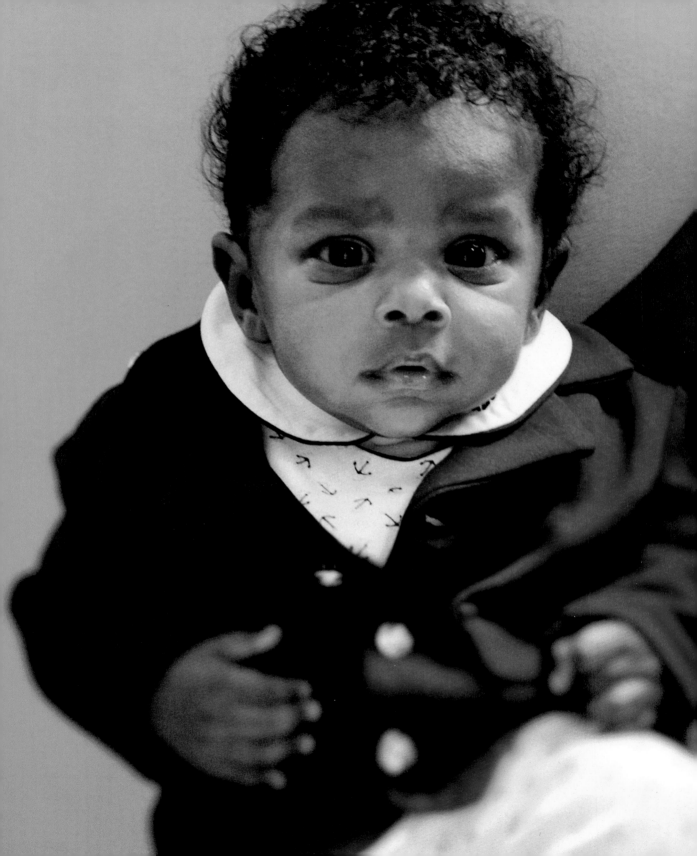

DEDICATION

To my grandson

MASTER KING JAY WATSON

You are God's gift to your parents and a blessing to me! I know without a shadow of a doubt that you will take after your parents' incredible intelligence and travel the world. You will be fluent in multiple languages, an expert in reading, math and science, and an art connoisseur. And as long as I'm around, you will always know timeless fashion as well!

TABLE OF CONTENTS

INTRODUCTION

As far back as I can remember, all of the men in my life dressed to the nines and had an eye for fashion. The women in my family were stylish and always looked great too! My granddad on my dad's side had a coat, shoe, belt, and hat fetish. My granddad on my mom's side always had a suit on no matter the occasion—period. He didn't believe in being underdressed. His philosophy was that it was always better to be prepared for anything that came his way. In his mind, a fitted suit, dress shoes, and fedora never failed.

My dad also loves clothes. While I was growing up, I especially remember his love for leather and suede jackets. He had way too many to count. As former military, it was in my dad and granddad's DNA to be sharply dressed and dapper all the time. Interestingly enough, my father-in-law is former military as well and has the same mindset— being underdressed is never an option. Regardless of the family outing or event, I have vivid memories of my dad dressed in either suits and ties or a sports jacket to give his outfit a level of formality he always desired. Even at 76-years-young, you won't find him without a sharp blazer, even if it's paired with comfortable jeans and Chelsea-styled boots.

While in junior high school, eighth grade to be exact, I had the choice of taking a typing class or a sewing class. I knew that the sewing class was right up my alley. I always wanted to design my own clothes and I figured that if I learned how to sew, I would be well on my way to doing that. As a bonus, one of my good buddies, Darryl Bradley, who also loved fashion, took the class with me.

One of my first projects in sewing class was to design my own polo-style shirt. I can remember being inspired by one of my then-favorite designers, Izod Lacoste. I patterned my exclusive Troy Boston polo shirt after his style. Darryl, meanwhile, styled his shirt after Ralph Lauren's iconic polo shirt. For my part, I remember gently removing the green gator from a pair of my favorite white Lacoste socks and sewing it onto a plain cobalt blue polo style shirt. You couldn't convince me that my shirt wasn't an official Lacoste shirt. Everything about my design seemed legit!

From that day to this, I've been particular about style and fashion. I still can hear my school teachers commenting on my style of dress and how different it was from those of my schoolmates across grade levels. I often wore khakis, bucks, and leather jackets to school. I hardly wore what most of my peers wore—sweats, jeans, and tennis shoes. Not that there's anything wrong with sweats, jeans, and sneakers. That was my uniform on the weekends. However, during the school week, I wanted to dress well and wear nice clothes. Even though I had a keen eye for fashion and enjoyed my sewing class, one of the primary reasons Darryl and I chose sewing over typing was because there was an overwhelming amount of girls in the sewing class. In fact, the class was almost 80 percent girls versus 20 percent boys, if that. We convinced ourselves we were being strategic and fantasized about how this class would further increase our popularity in school and around our neighborhood. It seemed like a brilliant idea to us back then. I'm not sure if it actually paid off as we had imagined, but we certainly learned a lot about sewing in the process.

My Lacoste fixation notwithstanding, I've never really gotten caught up in trends. However, I do consider myself a risk-taker when it comes to men's fashion. Every now and again I'll add a piece to my closet that may be considered trendy, but overwhelmingly the clothes in my closet are deemed classic and timeless fashion wear. As a result, I'm frequently asked about my style of dress and sought after for input on creating ensembles. One thing that used to annoy me back in the day but now simply makes me laugh is when someone compliments my outfit or style of dress and then asks if my wife dressed me or purchased the specific item they admire. I remember how I used to respond with sort of an attitude, "I'm a grown man and can dress myself." The funny thing is, while my wife, Vicky, has an insanely talented eye for men's fashion and often picks up nice additions to my wardrobe, she doesn't get the credit for my innovative creations. Although, I most certainly give her credit for the many incredible items that she's added to my wardrobe over the past 30 years, she doesn't lay out my clothes—and never has. She also doesn't "dress me," as would sometimes be alluded to by the backhanded compliments received from others. Ok, I just had to get that off of my chest. We can now proceed.

My family and the young men that I mentor who admire my style of dress motivated me to share my thoughts on men's fashion in the form of a book. You'll learn in subsequent chapters that my style is very dependent on the appropriate "hardwear" accompanying each ensemble. Commonly referred to as accessories, hardwear, as I call them, can really make or break an outfit. We'll spend ample time discussing hardwear and its importance. Throughout the book, I'll insert a few side bars here and there, all full of nuggets, aha moments, or just good-to-know info to add to your knowledge regarding men's fashion. If you're looking to spice up your existing wardrobe, shake it up a bit by taking it from good to great, slightly revamp it, or try something completely new without breaking the bank, this book is for you!

In the pages of this book, you'll get to meet the following models: Masters Audré Dabney (my godson) and Phelan Harry II; young adults Robert (Rob) Murray III (my nephew), Trevon Barnes, Patrick Wade, Barrington Little and, the one and only Cliff Johnson. Each, regardless of age, background, upbringing, and life experience has a sense of style that I absolutely admire. They take personal pride in their appearance and always strive to look and be their very best selves. In the chapters to come, you'll be able to learn from their insights while observing their style.

No matter what adjustments you decide to make to your closet, whether you add, subtract or change how you wear your items, always remember that you have to be comfortable and confident in what you wear every day. I dare you to be you.

Ready to elevate your style? Let's go.

> *"Looking good isn't self-importance; it's self-respect."*
>
> *Charles Mix*

CHAPTER 1 – FASHION DEFINED

Fashion can be defined in many ways. Fashion designer Rachel Zoe says, "Style is a way to say who you are without having to speak." Miuccia Prada suggests that "fashion is instant language."

Dictionary.com defines fashion as "a prevailing custom or style of dress, etiquette, or socializing; conventional usage in dress, manners especially of polite society, or conformity to it." Meanwhile, Webster's Dictionary simply defines it as "a popular way of dressing during a particular time or among a particular group of people, the business of creating and selling clothes in new style, and clothes that are popular."

When I think of fashion and its definition, I instantly think of having fun with my style of dress, as it almost feels like a form of art for me. More importantly, I think about being comfortable and confident in my own skin. Oftentimes, people emulate others' style of dress. However, when your body type isn't taken into consideration—such as height, weight, arm length, neck size, and other factors—what looks great on another person may not look great on you. As important as your style is, equally important is what you're physically comfortable wearing. I like to think that my wife looks greats in pant suits, skirt suits and business suits in general, however, she feels too stuffy and physically restricted in them. So she leans more toward dresses and coordinates such as blazers with skirts or pants, depending on her mood. When you

feel great and look great, it helps to build confidence.

The models pictured throughout this easy-to-read guide on timeless fashion all have one thing in common—they each know what works for, and looks good on, their specific body type. Whether you're six feet tall or have an 18-inch neck, you need to wear clothes that fit, complement your body type, and showcase your personality. As one would imagine, there are all types of myths out there and I will do my best to address the most common such as when you are a bigger frame, just wear bigger clothes. This is a big no-no. Keep reading and it will be addressed.

Our men's apparel model Rob suggests that fashion is what you buy, but your style is how you leverage your apparel to show off your best assets while reflecting your personal style. Further, Rob maintains that while particular fashions may come to an end, one's sense of style lasts forever. He further acknowledges that your choice of style will introduce you to the room before you even have a chance to speak—so choose wisely. That's pretty powerful! Lastly, Rob is a firm believer that self-confidence is the best outfit and that one should rock it and own it. BAM—this is profound for sure. For me, simply put, fashion is what you wear and style is how you wear it. Be sure to wear it well.

Take a moment and think about how you define fashion. Has your definition evolved over time depending on your life circumstances?

Someone who I've always looked up to and admired for a variety of reasons is my Uncle Buck Dabney. He has sports coats and shoes in his possession that are older than I am, but still look brand new and timeless. Why and how can that be? Easy, he buys well-made items and takes great care of them. For example, he resoles his shoes as often as needed. Therefore, they last.

When discussing men's fashion with others, there's an issue that frequently comes up: whether or not to monogram your dress shirts. I think the answer is quite simple: It's completely up to you. How liberating! If you choose to monogram, most stylists recommend you keep the letters to a maximum of three initials and use a font that is easy to read. It's also suggested that you keep the size of the initials to about a quarter-of-an-inch. At this point, I haven't monogrammed any of my dress shirts but may give it a spin in the near future, as I continuously look to spice up my own wardrobe.

When you buy quality pieces made of durable materials—whether shoes, suits, belts, or wallets—such as Italian leather, your priceless items really have the ability and propensity to last a lifetime. I can remember in my early twenties, my fashion was heavily dependent on workout gear and tennis shoes as I was spending a lot of time coaching young boy's basketball. Even though most of my discretionary time was spent in the gym, I was still mindful of and intentional about my dress. I've learned over the years that there is always someone watching you and looking up to you. I wanted to be sure that the young boys that I was responsible for coaching and providing leadership to (and their parents and teachers), had a great example of how to not only conduct themselves on and off the basketball court, but also, how to appropriately dress in the gym. Believe it or not, there really is a way to dress for exercise without looking sloppy and unappealing.

For example, if you're unable to keep your white athletic socks crisp and sparkling clean, try wearing black athletic socks instead. Take a couple of minutes and wipe the dust off of your sneakers. Most can be thrown in the washer and dryer or can even air dry. In need of new sneakers but short on cash at the moment? Purchase a pair of fresh laces for less than $5 to spruce up your existing kicks. Just like a fresh coat of paint does wonders for a room, a fresh pair of socks and shoelaces do wonders for older sneakers. Concerned about your physical shape or appearance in the gym? Spanx actually makes fitted undergarments for men to help us suck it in too! The bottom line is this: take pride in your appearance regardless of the environment or situation.

I like to think that my wife is very fashionable and has in her closet a wide selection of outfits to suit any event. The interesting thing I've noticed is that she has a few go-to outfits that she feels most comfortable wearing.

MEN'S HARDWEAR

1. What's your go-to outfit? Is there something in your closet that you instantly think of wearing when you're invited out or have an important meeting scheduled? If so, what is it? Describe it here.

....

....

....

....

2. Now think about your feet. What kinds of shoes do you wear most often? Soft bottom, hard bottom, rubber sole? Do you tend to wear fun socks that are loud, solid, print, patterned? Take a moment and inventory your shoe collection, what patterns are you noticing? List them here.

....

....

....

....

....

....

....

....

3. What's the one item in your closet that you just can't part with, no matter how old, worn, potentially outdated or just plain too small? For me, it's the tweed wool Ralph Lauren paperboy style hat I bought in 1989, the same year my daughter was born. I still wear it today and I can't imagine ever donating it or giving it away. Maybe, just maybe, I'll let my grandson have it when he's old enough to rock it well and, most importantly, appreciate it. List the most special item in your closet here.

....

....

....

....

4. In the next chapter, we will discuss how to identify clothing that fits properly and complements your body's shape. How would you describe your current or desired body type? Athletic, stocky, muscular? Thin, heavy set, average? Short waist, long torso, standard proportions? At five feet five inches tall, I consider myself a few inches shy of average height and on the stocky side. I have a thick neck (17 inches) and broad shoulders, so I pay particular attention to the shirt collars and ties I wear. I like to ensure that the combined spread (width, cut, etc.) of the two complement my size and style. Describe your body type here.

....

....

5. When putting together outfits, do you often mix and match your clothes or generally play it safe by strictly adhering to matched sets or colors? I have evolved in this area over time. I will admit that for far too long my style was what my wife refers to as *matchy-matchy*; I very seldom stepped out of the box to mix and match. Now I find myself mixing and matching far more often than playing it safe. I have fun in the process. Mixing and matching has proven to be liberating, but remember that at the end of the day, it's always best to do what makes you most comfortable and confident in your dress. Where do you shake out? Flesh it out here.

....

....

....

....

....

....

6. To accessorize or not? That's the question. How much time do you spend accessorizing your ensemble? How's your watch, belt, cuff link, bracelet, sock, pocket square, necktie, bow tie, and overall hardwear game? For the longest time, I shied away from certain accessories like pocket squares and bracelets. Now I have a blast with colorful beaded bracelets and pocket squares that rarely match my shirt and tie/bow tie. This is another topic that we'll discuss in greater detail later in the book. For now, what are your thoughts about accessories and how do you make them work for you? Take a moment and journal it here.

....

....

....

....

....

7. How do you organize your closet and clothes overall? Do you hang your dress shirts by color? It's often said that how a man organizes his clothes and closet impacts his ability to be most creative when crafting an ensemble. The thought behind this is that if your closet is disorganized (clothes hung with no rhyme or reason, etc.) your outfits will appear disorganized when you put them on. Close your eyes and get a good visual of your closet. What do you see?

....

....

....

....

....

....

....

....

....

....

....

....

....

....

....

....

....

"Clothes and manners do not make the man; but when he is made, they greatly improve his appearance."

Arthur Ashe

CHAPTER 2 – CLOTHES THAT FIT

Jeremy Reeves, owner of fashion website Kinowear.com, which has been visited by more than 40,000 men seeking to upgrade their style, has some quick tips. One of his tips regarding the importance of size is: Fit is king. I couldn't agree more.

I have to admit that I'm frequently disturbed when I see men in clothes that do not fit properly, whether it's a sizing issue or just a bad fit for their specific body type. Jeremy shares that one of the most important ways to improve your style is by wearing clothes that don't just fit, but fit impeccably. I'm in complete agreement but unfortunately, I see way too many guys in clothing that are sizes upon sizes too big. Likewise, I don't like to see men wearing clothes that are obviously too small. That said, I'm a raving fan of wearing clothes that truly fit the shape and size of my body type .

So how do you know the proper clothing size for your body? I'm so glad that you asked. If I were you, I would take an hour or so on your next day off and make it a point to visit a major department store that sells men's clothing. Even if you do not end up purchasing clothes from that particular store or men's boutique, shops like Saks Fifth Avenue, Nordstrom and Neiman Marcus all have personal stylists on site who delight in helping shoppers—for free. They will accurately measure you for suits, shoes, dress shirts, and more. They also recommend items that would look best on you. Once you're armed with this priceless intel, you'll instantly become dangerous and prepared to take on the fashion world. We know that applied knowledge is power so once you have your sizes noted, it's off to the races.

Rob frequently reminds those he mentors that whether it's on a big or small frame, there's nothing like wearing a well-fitted, well-made tailored suit. As a fairly big guy with a large frame, he used to shy away from clothes that actually fit. He was convinced at one point that he needed to wear oversized clothes to compensate for his larger frame and overall weight. It wasn't until after he was measured for a tailored suit and wore it with mega confidence, that he was inundated with compliments about his appearance.

While being professionally fitted for the suit, Rob learned several things from the experts. I'll share some of them with you now and more later on in this book. Rob learned about a tailor's measurements and he learned details about pants. Flat front trousers gave him a slimmer and more luxurious look. Pleated pants offered a looser fit. Pants with pinstripes gave the appearance of elongation. Next, he learned that the purpose of the buttons on the outside sleeve of a suit jacket was to allow the wearer to unbutton and roll up his sleeves when washing his hands. Thus, the fabric remained dry. Lastly, he wanted to know about pure wool suits. When should they be worn? He queried the tailor and did additional research. Rob learned that there are seasons for wool and seasons for ultra-lightweight wool, according to the experts at Kilgour. A high-end and highly regarded men's apparel shop, Kilgour is on London's famed Savile Row. As Rob shared his research and what he learned from this experience with me, I was quite proud and reflected how I was nearly twice his age before I knew all of this!

The bottom line is that, like Rob, you should take the necessary time to be properly fitted and learn your actual size. Learn how to wear a fitted

MEN'S HARDWEAR

suit well. You will find, like Rob, that this makes you look better and feel more confident.

The book *Art of Style: Fashion for the Everyday Man* details three basic fits. The first is a very loose fit that leaves way too much room in the clothes; this fit does not complement any man's body type. The second is a tight fit, which is the complete opposite of the loose fit. Here, there may be skin bulging through the buttons on the shirt. In the case of tight pants, the man's pant seam may actually tear when he sits down. Obviously, this fit is probably the worst of them all. The third is the right fit. It exists when the clothing simply complements a man's body and really conforms to his body type, without restriction of movement or cause for alarm when walking, sitting, bending down, or raising arms.

If you fasten your shirt collar, you should be able to breathe normally and not turn colors! No outline of your own shoulder should appear in the sleeve (in which case the suit is too small), and the sleeves should never sag (in which case the suit is too big). There shouldn't be any creases or ripples radiating from a fastened button. If there are, adjust the size as necessary. Lastly, the bottom hem of the jacket should be level with the knuckles of your hand.

Our model Patrick Wade featured on page 30 has a keen eye for fashion and as you may suspect, fashion that fits and complements. He often reminds me that the fabric of an item is critically important. Not all fabrics feel good on everyone's skin or hangs the way it's intended. Factors like one's body type affect this. Patrick is quick to advise others who are interested in improving their fashion game to consider each garment's fabric, fit, and quality. Patrick believes that the clothes should be made of a fabric that is comfortable against your skin and has a natural flow of movement. He's a strong believer that the clothes you wear should accentuate your physical assets and be functional.

Not only should we be concerned with the proper fit of our suits, sports coats, trousers, and dress shirts, but we should have a well-fitted undershirt as well. Speaking of undershirts, did you know that there are varying types of undershirts? My favorites are the black and grey crew neck style undershirts, but it's good to also have the white crew neck, white V-neck, and, occasionally, a white tank top handy. I like the black because of its versatility. It can easily be worn solo, under a nice fitted jacked, which is why it's important that the undershirt be fitted as well and not baggy and too big. The grey is good as it doesn't show up under my dress shirts from some of the bolder color families. The crew neck in general ensures everything that needs to be covered is covered and helps protect the armpits of the dress shirt. The V-neck undershirt disappears when wearing a shirt that you may want to wear unbuttoned at the top. It also helps protect the armpits of the shirt that is worn over top. The tank top is good to wear under T-shirts. Essentially, all styles of undershirts should be soft on the body and fit like your second skin.

Why so much fuss over clothes that fit and, more importantly, fit your body type? It's really simple. Your style of dress and how you show up every day is your marketing tool. Your appearance is everything and it will speak for you, in a variety of settings, before you're ever given the opportunity to speak for yourself. Well-dressed, well-kempt and well-groomed men all seem to understand that the style and fit of one's clothes absolutely matters.

Side note: It's good to remind ourselves how critically important it is to pay attention to and take note of our dress and overall appearance when interviewing. I am a strong believer that a job applicant's outward appearance can be more determinative in his getting a job offer than his resume or interviewing skills. I certainly don't want to leave my career and future opportunities to chance based on a wardrobe misstep and I suspect that you don't either.

Interestingly enough, there are countless articles online and in magazine print that strongly encourage men and women to stop wearing clothes that just don't fit their specific body type—to include shape, size and height. Check out www.RealSimple.com and the article entitled "The Right Clothes for Your Body Type" for additional tips and suggestions. It's even suggested by some that it's actually hard to dress well because

I recently read pointers from Esquire The Biggest Black Book Ever: A Man's Ultimate Guide to Life and Style. *They detailed how men can know if their suits fit properly. I summarized the following tips that work for me and may be helpful to you.*

As it relates to the bottom of your pants, it's suggested that only a little cloth should ever drape over your shoes; ask your tailor for a one-inch break in the front crease. For shirts, a quarter- to half-an-inch of your shirt cuff should always be visible. Any more suggests that your sleeves are too long. As for jackets, the collar of your jacket should neither stand away from nor conceal your shirt collar at the back of the neck.

MEN'S HARDWEAR

it takes work and not all of us are willing to put in the work. Imagine that.

Fit matters too. Like many, I wanted a promotion on the job, respect in my community, and the best relationships possible with family and friends. Wearing clothes that fit had a huge part to play in my ability to accomplish it all, not to mention to be able to display the confidence needed. I realized very early in life by watching the examples set by my father, uncles and grandparents, that when I really took my appearance seriously, others took me seriously. Conversely, society sometimes discounts individuals based on appearance, before they've had a chance to articulate a thought. Whether or not it's fair or just, it's still the reality.

Ask yourself what story you want your appearance to tell on your behalf. I think most of us have heard the saying that you only have one chance to make a first impression. What assumptions will be made about you based on the way you show up in a room? We've already talked about confidence as an added benefit of dressing well. We know too that confidence yields far-reaching personal gains. Fashion designer Edith Head reminds the style-savvy, "You can have anything you want in life if you dress for it."

When clothes shopping for various looks, consider some of the rules of the road—whether you're a bigger and taller man like model Barrington Little pictured on pages 22 and 29, or you have another body type. I have found these basic principles helpful in pulling together both ensembles and entire wardrobes.

If you are lean like model Patrick Wade (page 30), feel free to explore horizontal lines, as they create a broader look. Go ahead, flaunt the three-button suit jacket or cardigan sweater that accentuates the torso.

When considering types of wool clothing to wear, I let the actual temperature outside, rather than the seasonal clothing trends, guide me. I assume this is true for most folks. Take for instance this past spring in Washington, DC Most days felt more like winter. As a result, for most of April and May, I wore my heavier wool sports jackets instead of lighter weight jackets. I remember in mid-May Vicky and I attended a fundraiser gala downtown. It was so chilly and rainy that evening that she wore dress boots instead of heels with her cocktail dress!

In general, those with a lean build, regardless of height, should avoid wearing anything too big. If you're of a lean to average build, word on the fashion street is that you may want to avoid vertical lines; yet you may enjoy cuffed pants with shallow pleats.

For shorter and stockier men like myself, it's wise to avoid busy prints like the chalk stripes. Also, please stay far away from wide-leg pants, with or without pleats.

If you are of a larger build like model Rob Murray III (shown on page 33), consider the complementary appearance of straight-leg pants. For the bigger build, it's also a great idea to keep the ensemble simple, whether dressing casually, formally, or in business attire. Many times, wearing lots of mixed patterns and bold colors in the same outfit detracts from the overall look. Remember, regardless of body type, wearing complementary fabric patterns is as important in achieving a pulled-together look as wearing clothes that fit properly.

In my travels abroad, I've found it very useful when shopping to have a working knowledge of how to convert US sizes to European sizes, whether with shirts, pants, or shoes. I used to get pretty confused and frustrated when shopping at European stores. In the States, I was accustomed to looking for a size 40 or 42S suit but when abroad or shopping from European retailers online, I quickly learned that a 50 or 52S was the proper conversion for my US size. However, even with the help of conversion charts, sometimes you just have to try the clothes on because, depending on the cut, the listed size may or may not fit you. The following pages include sizing charts that you may find helpful.

MEN'S HARDWEAR

MEN'S CLOTHING

US/UK	EURO	CM
36	46	91
38	48	97
40	50	102
42	52	107
44	54	112

MEN'S SHIRTS

US/UK	CM
14	37
15	38
15	39.5
16	41
16	42
17	43
17	44

MEN'S SHOES

US	UK	EU	JAPAN
7	6 1/2	39	25
8	7 1/2	41	26
9	8 1/2	43	27.5
10 1/2	10	44	28.5
11 1/2	11	45	29.5

Time to take inventory of what's in your closet if you haven't done so this quarter. It's a good idea to do this often, quarterly at the very minimum. I try to make this a monthly habit as things accumulate fast. However, I must admit that monthly doesn't happen as often as I would like. So again, try to take inventory and purge every three months. Remember that it's not just the clothing and shoes that need to be inventoried and purged but also the accessories that have been added to the wardrobe that may no longer serve a purpose.

I also have a rule that Vicky and I both adhere to (or should I say, try to adhere to) and it is that when we add something new to our wardrobes, we donate a minimum of three items to Goodwill and/or those we mentor and in whom we make investments. We've both been guilty of holding onto clothes, shoes, accessories, and more that we know deep down inside we will not wear again. Still, we struggle with some form of emotional attachment for whatever reason. Sometimes, we're really good at giving away items and simply letting something go. If the items are too big, too small, not our style any longer, or if we just want to be a blessing to someone who may have expressed interest in the item. We tend to challenge ourselves in that if we haven't worn it within a year— two years for seasonal items—it's probably a good idea to let it go.

A word of caution, if you own a rare find, something of significance that can never be replaced, something vintage or an article passed down from a loved one, do take a moment to think through whether this is something you really want to give away. Vicky had a leather tote bag that she received as a gift in high school. It was very well made, made in Italy in fact, had detailed stitching which made the bag pop and was in fairly good condition. While cleaning out her closet one day she noticed that it had been years since she had used it and she decided to part with it. She has regretted that decision ever since. While the brand of the bag is still in business, that particular style from the 80s

is nowhere to be found. She's searched high and low, checked online, and scoured consignment and thrift stores—she has yet to come across it! Darn it! There is a fine line, a delicate balance, between just hanging on to everything when you know most will never be worn again, and holding on to something of sentimental value or that is irreplaceable. Please learn from us and examine your prospective donations carefully. Here's the deal, once you decide to give it up, let it rip and have no regrets. No need to look back; you're not going that way!

Take a moment now to list those things in your closet that you know you will never wear again and make a commitment to donate them and bless someone else today. How about you go beyond just committing to donate and while listing your items also write a date by which you will have them out of your home. If it's been a while, you may want to work over four weekends and categorize your inventory and donations by date (i.e. first round is shoes, next batch is clothes, third weekend is accessories, and on the fourth and final weekend, all remaining items go). If you don't make the task manageable, it may seem overwhelming and result in you taking no action at all.

....

....

....

....

....

....

....

MEN'S HARDWEAR

....
....
....
....
....
....
....
....
....

> *"Dressing well is a form*
> *of good manners."*
>
> *Tom Ford*

MEN'S HARDWEAR

CHAPTER 3 – CLASSIC BLACK

The book titled *Nordstrom Guide to Men's Style* lists the following as wardrobe must haves:

- 5 suits
- 5 sports coats
- 5 trousers (dress)
- 3 pants (casual)
- 15 shirts
- 10 ties
- 4 pairs of shoes (lace up, loafer, boot, and canvas)
- 4 belts that complement the shoes above
- Socks, underwear, and T-shirts
- 4 pairs of jeans (black, dark blue, washed, and lived-in)
- Tuxedo and accoutrements
- 10 pieces of knitwear (3 crew necks, 3 V-necks, 2 vests, and 2 cardigans)
- 5 fun sports shirts
- 5 great t-shirts

Let's admit, this list is pretty robust and acquiring five suits may be a longer-term goal for many men. However, let's also admit that it would be a huge success if every man owned at least one really good classic black suit, as modeled by Cliff Johnson. Meanwhile, *Esquire's Black Book* recommendations for a functional wardrobe include the following: a minimum of three suits, four ties, five shirts, two pairs of shoes, and one overcoat. Again, I would add to this list—and strongly suggest you do too—a classic black suit.

Consider this, the classic black suit can be worn in multiple ways and has the most versatility. With the right accessories, the classic black suit can be worn in at least five different settings—formal, semi-formal, cocktail/festive, business, and casual. Let's take a peep at each one.

1. Formal. Also known as black tie, it refers to attire inclusive of tuxedoes for men and long gowns for women. However, if accessorized appropriately, the classic black suit is absolutely acceptable for an event requiring formal wear. You will find that formal dress is required at many gala events, evening weddings, receptions and the like.

   Famed designer Tom Ford has a rule for men and it's to always keep your dinner or formal jacket buttoned, as it gives a finished look.

2. Semi-formal. Also referred to as after-five attire, it is very similar to Black Tie, however tuxedoes typically are not expected. The classic black suit—or classic black, as I like to refer to it—is always perfect for such an event. Semi-formal dress is the dress code for many charity events, corporate awards ceremonies and many weddings.

3. Cocktail/Festive. This attire is often requested at adult birthday parties, themed parties and holiday parties. The classic black, without a tie but with a fun pocket square for a pop of color, tends to work great.

4. Business. Although many companies have migrated from traditional business attire, business outfits are still de rigueur in many workplaces. As you might imagine, yes, the classic black does the trick. A great tie, crisp white shirt, fun socks, and shined shoes never fail. Tip: Keep a dark blazer in your office just in case you're wearing business-casual and need a quick style upgrade for an unexpected meeting. Having the classic black blazer on hand and ready for action can prevent panic and boost your confidence when you need it most.

5. Casual. This clothing is for date night, the company picnic, happy hour, weekend brunch and neighborhood gatherings. By the way, casual attire doesn't always mean jeans, T-shirts, and sneakers, although these items work. The classic black can be worn with a simple T-shirt, oxford shirt, or even a polo style shirt in a casual setting. Remember that the shoes you pick for the casual look matter. A nice pair of loafers or nice sneakers without socks will give your classic black the upscale casual look that you desire. You can always pair your black blazer jacket with a nice pair of dark denim jeans and you're set. One word of caution with casual dress, when you're unsure of the recommended attire, let casual be your last resort. It's always better to be overdressed than underdressed! When all else fails, pop a pocket square in with the classic black and take your style game to the next level.

In general, when wearing the classic black, I wear black on black—as in a black dress shirt and black tie or bowtie. I'm referring here to the kind you tie; NO clip-ons please! I may even throw in a black pocket square. You also have the option of wearing just the black shirt, buttoned up, with no tie. You can certainly accent the look with a subtle pocket square. Another option would be to wear a white oxford style shirt with a black bowtie or ascot and call it a day! Of course, you want to wear what makes you comfortable and confident when you walk in the room.

Remember, not all classic black suits are created equal, meaning not all are quality made, wear well, or last long. Model Patrick Wade strongly suggests that men invest in a classic black suit that holds up well to laundering or dry cleaning as needed and is soft to the touch. Keep in mind, high-end stores are not the only places to secure your quality classic black. Try visiting Marshalls, T.J. Maxx, Neiman Marcus' Last Call, Nordstrom Rack, Off Fifth, Hugo Boss and Giorgio Armani outlet stores, just to name a few. I once found a $750 super 150 Hugo Boss suit at Marshalls on clearance for only $100!

The terms super 100 or super 150 refer to the fitness of the wool thread. The higher the number, the better the wool is and the finer the thread will be. The number associated with super, such as 100, 120, 150, etc. doesn't suggest the suit itself is 100 percent wool. The inside label will list that, so be sure to take a look before making the investment.

You will notice that I talk a lot about bargains in this book. Why? Because the bargains are out there but you have to be willing to put a little work in to find them. Whether you're upgrading your closet with a new black suit or buying one for the first time, keep in mind that it's better to buy one really nice, all-season, mid-weight fabric suit that's good from summer through winter, than to buy two cheap, low-quality suits, any day of the week.

Even though we've focused on the classic black in this chapter, it's good to know that when you have one navy, one pattern, and one grey suit in your closet, in addition to your classic black, your wardrobe is essentially complete. They all mix and match very well and are completely versatile, so they can work for any occasion. Whether you own a classic black or another great suit, try really hard to resist dry cleaning your suits after every wear, as it destroys the fabric. In most cases, you can wear your suits five-plus times before they need to be professionally cleaned.

Take a moment and take inventory of your classic black suit (or suits). Make note of how you're currently wearing it and journal a few new ways that you can wear it in the future. Also write how you will accessorize it differently for various events.

....

....

....

....

....

....

....

....

"Walk like you have three men walking behind you."

Oscar de la Renta

CHAPTER 4 –
TREND ME NOT

It has been said that while all industries face change over time, the fashion industry has been known to change far more rapidly than any other industry. Therefore, it's important to avoid trends when building your classic and timeless wardrobe. Why? It's quite simple. If you chase after the trends, you're likely to regret it later. Put another way, it's best to avoid becoming attached to things that are temporary, as with trends. I most certainly have fallen for a few trends over the years. Some worked out but most ended up with a short shelf life. I can clearly remember in the early 90s when baggy jeans were in style. Oh my, when I look back at pictures from that era, I can't stop laughing at how crazy I looked! What was I trying to accomplish with that look? With my height and build, the trendy baggy jeans did nothing for me. As much as those jeans cost, had I gone for the classic fit, meaning buying jeans that were my actual size, perhaps, I would still have them today. As you can imagine, every pair of baggy jeans that I owned back then has been vanquished from my wardrobe of today!

When I reflect on the many bags of clothing and accessories that I've donated to charities over the years, I have a vivid memory of several questionable items. What in the world was I thinking at the point of purchase? By no means am I suggesting that trendy items shouldn't be considered or even added to your wardrobe. However, what I am suggesting is that you give some additional thought before adding something today that you may not want to wear tomorrow. Some of what I consider to be trendy buys from my past remain in my closet today. They include a few pairs of tennis shoes and maybe a few T-shirts here and there. Other than that, I try to stay clear of anything deemed trendy and focus on items that will likely have longevity in my wardrobe.

I once read an article in the *Business Insider* that talked about several things that men should remove from their closet and even burn! The title of the article really intrigued me as it was pretty easy to see where the writer was going just by looking at his examples. The one thing all of the items mentioned in the article had in common was that they were trendy items at one point in time and have since lost their usefulness or relevance. So it's not all bad having a few trendy pieces here and there. They can be somewhat fun, however, if the great majority of your closet is based on the latest trends, you may not see a return on your investment over time. I strongly recommend that no more than 20 percent of your wardrobe include trendy items. There's no need to waste time or money shopping for anything that may not be worn a few months or years later. Famous fashion designer, Karl Lagerfield said "Trendy is the last stage before tacky." I believe there is a ton of truth in that quote. In fact, the older I get, the more I appreciate what my dad, granddads and father-in-law taught me years ago regarding timeless and classic fashion.

Model and fashion designer Trevon Barnes, seen on page 45, is a youthful 24-year-old and already values the timeless and classic look. Let's analyze his ensemble in the picture. His suit is a classic two-button suit. The shade of blue isn't too bold, but just right to pair with a variety of shirts, ties, pocket squares, cuff links, socks, and shoes. Notice the sophisticated look of his tie clip to keep his tie in place as he walks and moves around. His brown shoes have a distressed look at the toe, which adds pizzazz. The patterned dress shirt works well with the patterned purple tie. You will notice that the pocket square is also

patterned. The individual pieces complement each other while avoiding the trap of appearing rigidly color-matched. If you look carefully, you'll notice Trevon is wearing a fun pair of socks too. Overall, this ensemble is put together well. The model is very comfortable in it and clearly exudes confidence. Trevon is dressed well; this grants him access to many rooms and a seat at many tables at which he otherwise may have been denied had he been dressed differently.

While this model and fashion designer has some trendy items in his lineup, he knows the benefits of keeping the bulk of his closet filled with quality-made items that will stand the test of time. He shows zero hesitation when it comes to investing in timeless pieces, even when the price tag may appear to be a little steep. He realizes right now, that if taken care of, cleaned and stored properly, his investment will yield dividends over time. When asked where he gets so much wisdom about men's fashion at such a young age, he advised that he closely observed successful men that he admired while growing up and continues even today. These men dressed the part and Trevon determined that he would too. His parents are stylish as well, so Trevon's eye for fashion was inevitable. And just like he replicated the timeless fashions he observed, so too are a younger generation of middle and high school students. These mentees follow his example by dressing well and presenting themselves as cosmopolitan gentlemen.

So, what's your take on trends? Where do you stand? The famous late designer Gianni Versace often spoke about his desire to break rules and barriers. He had a clear vision that avoided fashion fads. Coco Chanel was quick to remind her fans that she didn't do fashion, rather she was fashion. In other words, trends didn't dictate her style, instead she created trends. Where do you stand, do popular fashions define you or do you decide what items are worthy of being included in your wardrobe? What trendy items are in your closet today? Do you still wear them? Take inventory. Which should stay and which should quickly find another home? When confronted with trends, how will your shopping behavior change going forward?

....

....

....

....

....

....

....

....

> *"Don't be into trends. Don't make fashion own you, but you decide what you are, what you want to express by the way you dress and the way you live."*
>
> *Gianni Versace*

CHAPTER 5 – HARDWEAR

My late grandfather, Everett Spillman, used to remind me as a young man that only when the pants of a great suit properly break and fall onto a pair of well-made shoes, coupled with the right accessories, then and only then is there a conversation of a somewhat perfect outfit.   Bottom line—accessories matter!

The business of fashion, inclusive of accessories, is a multi-billion-dollar global industry. Essentially, it's big business and I can clearly see why. My wife used to say, "no naked devices" when joking around with her former retail sales team in the wireless industry. It was a reminder to add value to customers' purchases by helping them accessorize their wireless devices with cases, covers, screen protectors, wireless speakers, athletic/fitness gear, and so much more. According to the industry experts, at that time, this was a $7 billion-dollar industry. My wife was helping the team promote accessories for wireless devices. In my mind, the concept is no different as it relates to one's wardrobe. I say, "no naked ensembles." I believe wearing accessories with any outfit helps to complete the look. Rocking varying accessories that you truly enjoy, helps bring your personality to life and can really make the difference between a nice outfit and a jaw-dropping one. Sometimes less is more and simple is really profound. Before we go too far, let's take a moment and define what I'm referring to as men's hardwear, or commonly known as accessories.

Dictionary.com defines accessory as "an article or set of articles of dress, as gloves, earrings, or a scarf, that adds completeness, convenience, attractiveness, etc., to one's basic outfit." Merriam-Webster.com defines it as "something added to something else to make it more useful, attractive, or effective."

When I envision accessories, a few things come to mind such as bright but tasteful socks, a well-made belt, wrist wear (otherwise known as a nice timepiece or watch), a fun beaded bracelet to add a pop of color, a well-made tie, a colorful, non-matching pocket square, and my favorite dog tag on a titanium necklace as shown below.

MEN'S HARDWEAR

Even at the precious age of 3-months-old, my grandson, Master King Jay Watson, has been introduced to some necessary hardwear. His items include a bib, functional belt, rain boots for inclement weather, baby aviator sunglasses, bucket hat when hiking with his dad, fun socks, his favorite book and more!

GROOMING

While we're on the topic of accessories, please note that you can have the best wardrobe on the planet, paired with the best accessories, but without intentional grooming, inclusive of a great cologne that complements your natural scent, and a regular fitness regimen, it may not pay the dividends expected in any area of your life. Be sure to keep your hands and feet manicured, either at home or professionally. Keeping a nail file, nail clipper, and hand/feet moisturizer handy is critically important to your overall appearance so be sure to add these to your accessory checklist.

As part of the grooming conversation, let's briefly discuss the art of shaving. While I didn't intend to sport a shiny, bald head for the past 25-plus years, it happened by default when I started losing my hair in my early 20s. The once thick, soft curls began to thin out and recede. I felt then and certainly now that my only option was to shave it all off. Fortunately, I have never struggled with razor bumps on my head or face. However, I am aware of their common causes, such as sensitive skin and curly hair that tends to curl back into the skin, rather than grow straight out of the skin. The good news is that there are ways to prevent the razor bump syndrome by either letting your hair grow and keeping it at a minimum 0.5 mm to 1 mm in length or investing in laser assisted permanent hair removal. If you are struggling with razor bumps, I highly recommend that you make an appointment with a dermatologist, as appearance is important.

I'm often asked how I keep my head smooth and what products I use. I've tried various over-the-counter products but the one brand that has worked for me for more than 10 years now is The Art of Shaving, which can be found at most department stores, online, and in boutique stores. I use their pre-shave oil or gel, unscented shaving cream, after shave balm with a three-blade razor and badger hair brush that sits nicely on the razor stand. Jack Black, Tom Ford, and Kiehl's all have great facial cleansers that I rely on as well. A few must-haves for me include a two-in-one Shea Moisture brand shampoo and conditioner. I typically use Kiehl's lip balm, their facial cleanser/exfoliator, facial moisturizer with built in SPF 20, and eye balm. For emergencies, I keep on hand Jack Black Bump Fix Razor Bump & Ingrown Hair Solution. Ensuring the bald head looks great and bump free starts and ends with the products and tools consistently used. Most, if not all, department stores have tons of samples of these brands, so grab a few and see what works best for you!

Finally, I highly recommend that you check out the book *Manmade:The Essential Skincare & Grooming Reference for Every Man*, by Chris Salgardo. There appears to be a gap in knowledge from generation to generation as it relates to skincare. Women tend to fill up the cosmetics and skin care counters but men tend to consume less. Five quick tips from the book *Manmade* are to add to your arsenal:

- Secure a great dermatologist.
- Apply sunblock every day regardless of skin pigmentation.
- Sharpen your dull straight razor on the bottom of your favorite ceramic mug.
- Use lip balm for more than dry lips, like to tame wild eyebrows.
- Use clear nail polish to temporarily hold the thread when you encounter an unexpected loose button.

Not a bad list to also add to your accessory arsenal.

Expert grooming coupled with a well-fitted suit and your charming personality are great. Add an incredible necktie to the ensemble and you are gold! As you endeavor to refine your appearance, remember that accessories, like neckties and bow ties, are integral to a finished look. In many ways, they are as important to a finished presentation as larger articles of clothing. Accessories help pull it all together. So, invest in quality pieces. We'll spend time finding bargains for accessories a little later, but right now I do want to challenge you to make the investment in well-made ties. This doesn't mean the tie has to be crazy expensive either. Most of the men that I know and probably those you know too, can bank on receiving a new tie for Father's Day and over the Christmas holidays. So, it's good for you and those who shop for you to understand that well-made ties simply last longer and lay flatter. Be sure to share this information with your loved ones!

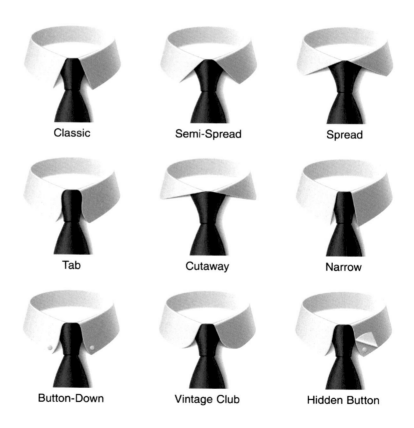

Classic	Semi-Spread	Spread
Tab	Cutaway	Narrow
Button-Down	Vintage Club	Hidden Button

MEN'S HARDWEAR

Now, in terms of the finished look, keep in mind that you can tie your neckties using different types of knots. As you decide which knot to go with for your ties, consider your neck size and your shirt collar. There are many collars from which to choose. See page 54 for examples of various types.

For example, four-in-hand tie knots can be neatly worn with all collar styles, while the Windsor knot is best for luxury and classic looks, coupled with a cutaway collar as shown on the chart; it is also the biggest and boldest knot of them all. Before I mastered the art of tying a bowtie, I watched YouTube videos and practiced until I perfected it. YouTube can be a great resource for you as well. There are tons of videos out there that compare the various tie knots and demonstrate how to tie each one. You can always stop by your nearby Nordstrom men's department. They have postcards that display each knot and show the steps to tie them.

Wearing quality ties and choosing complementary knots is just the beginning. You have many tie options available at your fingertips. Did you know that the tie family goes beyond the classic neckties and bow ties? It includes the cravat, which wraps around the neck but is not tied in a knot. There is also the ascot, a double-knotted tie that has one end draped over the other. The seven-fold tie is often folded by experts and has a thicker feel. It is made using a single piece of fabric that is literally folded seven times. The effect creates a larger looking tie knot with an incomparable drape. Due to the weight of a seven-fold tie, it is clearly differentiated from every other type of tie.

In addition to a variety of tie options, there are hosts of finishing accessories. These include scarves, suspenders—also known as braces— and of course pocket squares, which should never match the tie perfectly—sorry, I just couldn't resist. I'm thinking that every man

should have at least one of every type of these items in his collection, plus a classic necktie.

When the word "accessory" is used in the fashion world, men's accessories like the ties we've been discussing, are the first things that comes to mind. However, when I hear the word accessory, the first thing I think of is how a particular item can add value to my outfit or wardrobe in general. This is why I call my accessories hardwear. I jokingly coined the term because the great majority of my accessory collection consists of items like cuff links, watches, tie clips, and other such items made of glass, leather, metal, precious stones, or a combination thereof. Some other common accessories include things like wallets, business card holders, fun jewelry, like beaded bracelets, sunglasses, scarves, pocket squares, and even socks.

And about those socks, they absolutely matter! Don't believe the hype and by all means, avoid falling in the typical trap of having 20 pairs of black socks in your dresser drawer. Spend time and give real thought to which socks complement, enhance and finish off your outfit. Don't just grab the standard black socks.

I love how the book on fashion, entitled *Gentlemen*, by Bernard Roetzel insists accessories are those little things that make a big difference:

> "Man does not live from bread alone, and neither does style depend only on clothes. It is the small minor details, the accessories…those who are familiar with the language of accessories are not only capable of creating a more individual look, but can also interpret more from the outward appearance of those they are confronted with. The attention we devote to the relevant detail will improve our feel for the total look."

WALLETS

It's not a good look to have a wallet bulging out of any pocket, regardless of attire. There are men's wallets in the market designed to hold our most essential and valuable cards and cash without looking like we have a small brick in our pocket. And just as our female counterparts have multiple purses and wallets, it's perfectly okay for us to have a few nice wallets in our fashion repertoire as well. For years, I've watched my wife bounce between wallets and card cases depending on the size of her purse, shape of her bag, event she's attending, mood of the day or in rare cases, based on the color of the ensemble being worn. I've found with a lot of men, even with my own dad, we tend to hold on to our first wallets (you know, the nylon one or the one with Velcro). We were given them or purchased them at 16 as we entered manhood; and we never gave it up or upgraded to what I consider a respectable wallet. As you can guess, black and brown are the basic colors but it doesn't have to stop there. In the summer especially, it's perfectly fine to pull out a light colored wallet in the beige family, to wear with our light colored and light-weight suits. How about that fun, colorful wallet when heading off to a fun family vacation in the islands? Keep in mind, you can find great quality leather wallets and card holders for under $100. Not too long ago, as gifts for Father's Day, I purchased a Prada slim wallet/card case on sale for $87 and a similar men's one by Gucci for $110, both on clearance at Neiman Marcus. Both are very well made and, if taken care of by the recipients, will last for years.

It took me several years to liberate myself and invest in a few different wallets. I'm not suggesting we need ten or fifteen wallets hanging around to choose from, however it is nice to have a few options. Keeping the classic black and brown handy is a must, but having a couple of others can be fun. One of my favorite non-traditional wallets or card cases that

I've added to my collection is brick red in color, outfitted in crocodile skin and has just enough room for a few bills, driver's license, major credit card, and a few other critical cards, like my roadside assistance and health insurance cards. It's great on the weekends when I throw on a pair of jeans and am casually attired. Make an investment in a really nice wallet, even if it's your only one. There's nothing like being in an important meeting or event, you look your best, feel your best, and every detail regarding your attire, down to every accessory including the wallet, represents class. In that moment, the wallet just paid for itself seven times over. I believe men should thoughtfully consider and invest in all accessories, whether cuff links, watches, pocket squares, tie clips, or even pens. The little things add up and can really make a big difference.

WATCHES

Now let's shift gears and talk about one of my all-time favorite accessories—that would be watches, watches, and yes, more watches! What is it about the timepiece that gets me excited, you might ask? Is it the automatic movement, the one with an automatic wind? Is it the link or leather band design that gets me every time? Could it be the size of the face itself? For me, it's all of the above. I simply love watches and admire those with quality craftsmanship. After all of my many years of research on brands, models and designer histories, I'm drawn to the top brands known to most—Rolex, Breguet, Cartier, Omega, Hamilton, IWC, TAG Heuer, Breitling, and Baume & Mercier, just to name a few.

Speaking of watches and accessories, adding a quality watch winder to your collection is a wise investment. The watch winder helps watches with automatic movement retain accurate time even when you're not wearing them. A word of caution, please be certain if you decide to

It's not a bad idea to consider purchasing a belt hole-puncher, as your weight and waist size may fluctuate over time. The belt hole-puncher comes in thousands of shapes, sizes and strengths. It is designed to penetrate many materials such as leather, suede, etc. It's especially designed to neatly and uniformly add additional holes to your belt. This can protect the value of your belt collection investment. What's cool about belts made by designer Salvatore Ferragamo is that you can use regular household scissors to shorten his belts if they happen to be too big. Likewise, if you are shopping for a belt and happen to fall in love with a Ferragamo beauty and the store doesn't have your size but has a larger size, no worries. Buy it anyway, knowing you either can have the store itself cut the belt to fit your waist or take it home and do it yourself!

purchase a watch winder or already have one, that your winder is only running for a few minutes a day, preferably no more than thirty or forty minutes, to avoid damaging the winding mechanisms. I try to only travel with the watch that I'm wearing on my arm at the time, however, from time to time (no pun intended), I may have the need to bring another watch with me for a special occasion. When that happens, it's nice to have another watch accessory, called the watch roll, that not only stores the packed watch nicely but also helps to protect it from getting scratched from other items in your accessory bag and/or suitcase. Lastly, be sure to have your timepieces serviced as recommended. When it comes to having your watch repaired, should something go sideways, know your options. Of course, there is your local watch repair shop that typically takes a few days to do repairs. Most times, depending on the issue, it may take a week or so, but please be certain that your local spot is an authorized dealer of your brand of watch. Your watch brand's US headquarters is a nice option and what's really cool is when your watch is still under warranty, it's repaired at no additional cost to you. Then, there is always the opportunity to ship your valuable timepiece off to Switzerland where it will likely be cared for in a manner nearly indescribable. While this may be the best option, it's not always ideal as it's likely to take months to have it repaired and shipped back.

BELTS

Belts are another one of my favorite accessories. Belts can often be overlooked when building up the wardrobe or laying out an ensemble for any occasion, but shouldn't be. Like shoes and other critical accessories, belts matter. When buying your belt, go one size up from your waist size. For example, if your waist is size 34, snag the size 36 belt. You should be perfectly positioned for the middle hole since many

MEN'S HARDWEAR

belts have five holes pre-punched.

How do you pick the right belt to complement your look and keep your pants securely positioned around your waistline? Please do not waste your money on cheaply made belts. All leather belts aren't created equal, for example. Be sure to pay attention to the details and take a few minutes to examine the materials contained therein. Synthetic or leather look-a-likes have the look and feel of real leather of course, but fail to hold up to normal wear and tear. Bonded leather uses leather scraps and is typically better than synthetic, yet still not recommended. Belts described as 100 percent genuine leather generally suggest that the outer layer is genuine leather with the interior parts being made of leather scraps as mentioned earlier. That said, I believe that you can do better.

While I'm not a fan of too much matchy-matchy, I typically coordinate my belt color and material (or finish) with that of my shoes. Couturier Hardy Amies isn't a big fan of everything matching either. In an online article entitled "10 Lessons in Style from Hardy Amies," readers are advised that "to achieve the nonchalance which is absolutely necessary for a man, one article at least must not match." However, on some occasions, I will shake it up a bit. It just depends on the mood, the event, and what look I'm going for. In general if you're wearing a pair of black leather shoes, I would recommend that you keep it simple and pair up a black leather belt. In this scenario, the belt buckle may end up being your statement piece, depending on what look you're trying to achieve.

When considering the size, design, and finish of the belt buckle, it's wise to be mindful of the overall look of the outfit and the impact the buckle may have on it. Does it take away from the overall look? Is the buckle too bulky or big for the look you want? Regardless of the

There is the full-grain leather belt, which is considered top shelf. It's the highest quality of leather and has a tendency to stand the test of time. Belts made with full-grain leather do not use leather scraps or inferior materials. In general, cheaply made belts do not and will not last and you will end up spending more money replacing them over and over again. Take the plunge, make the jump and invest in quality. Investing in a few quality belts today can save you in the future. I personally have several belts that have lasted more than 10 years. Designers like Ferragamo, Hermes and others have belts and buckles that are interchangeable and even reversible. What's great about this versatility is that you can purchase a few belts and then instantly turn them in to many belt options. Fortunately, my wife budget, you can find a quality belt when you shop around—for as low as $30! Of course, some of the designer belts mentioned in this section, like a Ferragamo, can run into the hundreds of dollars so be sure to check the outlet stores for deep discounts. Remember, when you invest in a great reversible belt or one with an interchangeable buckle, it's like buying two for the price of one!

Next, keep in mind that some styles, such as belts made out of canvas material, shouldn't be paired with formal attire or a business suit. Of course, as with anything, there is a place for canvas belts, like with jeans, khakis and corduroys, for example.

I've been told by older men who've been in the fashion game a lot longer than I, that if I pair quality belts with one of the following six pairs of shoes, my belt-shoe collection will be set for three or more decades. They've witnessed it firsthand!

1. The cordovan lace up (preferably by Alden) can be found in stores like J.Crew and at high-end department and shoe stores around the world.

2. The wingtip is a classic. I prefer the Church's brand, which happens to be owned by Prada. Whether Church's or another brand, you can bank on the fact that this style of shoe likely will never expire or go out of style.

3. The Cap-toe shoe is timeless. I recommend the Crockett & Jones (C&J) brand. C&J has been making shoes since 1879. With proper care and storage, this brand promises to last the original owner a lifetime. Wow!

4. Double monk-strap shoes are my personal favorites. I highly recommend the John Lobb brand as being one of the best. In fact,

MEN'S HARDWEAR

at the time I was writing this chapter, the John Lobb chapel double monk-strap shoe was sold out on Neiman Marcus.com.

5. The penny loafer is well-known and worn by many. Because of my instep and shape of my foot, this style shoe, regardless of the designer, doesn't really work for me. However, word on the street has Salvatore Ferragamo leading the pack in this style shoe. Ferragamo is so classy that their penny loafer can be paired with a suit or a pair of shorts.

6. Berluti's wholecut boot. What's interesting about this style is that the boot is made from one piece of leather, which is not easy to do. Just ask any shoe maker! Berluti is known for being one of, if not the best, and most experienced. In fact, with the company's 120 years of experience, I certainly recommend their boot as a wardrobe staple.

As you can see, there are many moving parts when it comes to accessorizing your fine garb and they are all interrelated. Clearly, the shoes matter just as much as the accessories! In fact, it all matters.

CUFF LINKS

Even though small in size, they can make a big statement. In some cases, cuff links may not even be visible, however, the one wearing them knows they are there. Common cuff links are flat. They can be made of various metals, to include silver and gold. They are available in a variety of colors, like gray tones, navy or dark blues and the classic wine-hued red. Of course, if you're seeking bolder colors or an added variety of them, you can always have fun with fabric knots. They are a type of cuff link often on display near the checkout counter where dress shirts are sold. Then there are the more traditional metal cuff links, that can be fun. Wearers can express various hobbies and likes, such as cars, golf clubs, food items, etc. The key is to wear cuff links with dress shirts that have double cuffs and dress shirts that do not have buttons, making it obvious for the need of a cuff link. Believe it or not, fabric cuff links are pretty popular. Again, it can't be said enough, when considering any accessory to your outfit, be certain that you are comfortable with it. Always shy away from trying to be like someone else.

A few more items to consider adding to your hardwear tool kit that may be helpful include the following:

LINT BRUSH

How many times have you left the house looking clean and ready to face the world just to arrive at an important meeting or event covered in lint from your cashmere scarf or car seat? Don't let lint ruin your day! Arm yourself with at least three must-have weapons and always have them handy. First, invest in a quality lint brush and be sure to keep it clean to prevent it from clogging. Next is the infamous lint roller, it's good to have a spare in your suitcase, car and office. The sticky paper will grab everything off of your clothing. Beware, the cheaper lint rollers may leave behind a slight residue, so test them out on a small and unnoticeable area first. Lastly, you'll need a clothes brush. The clothes brush will go deeper in the fabric than the other two previously mentioned items, and will help lengthen the life of your garments.

SHOE TREES AND MORE

Another great accessory and tool of the trade to help keep your shoes looking good is the shoe tree. It is a great investment. It holds the shape of the shoe and can help to extend the life of your shoes. The shoehorn helps prevent ruining the back of the shoe and helps you to slide into your shoes with greater ease and comfort. A polishing kit will always do the trick when you're unable to indulge in a professional shoe shine. Black, brown and neutral polishes should take care of the great majority of your shoe collection.

DEALING WITH STAINS

Stains, stains and more stains! Rather than becoming frustrated or defeated, know some of the proven tricks of the trade. First, remember that you must never rub stains. Blot them instead, just as you would a stain or spill on your carpet. Blot, blot and blot. Rubbing deepens the stain and embeds it further into whatever fabric it is on. This makes it that much more difficult to get out. Time is of the essence, so move with speed to address the spill or stain. Some of the common stains like coffee, tea or latte, can be removed with white vinegar. (This is my sister-in-law, Dana McCoy's, favorite remedy.) I've been told that peroxide or club soda work miracles too.

Then there's the dreaded ink stain that drives you wild. No fear! Get the rubbing alcohol out, but remember not to rub, but blot instead. Hairspray has been rumored to help. Whichever you use, hand-wash the stain with a little detergent before having the shirt laundered or washing it in the machine at home. Lipsticks stains? While how you arrived at a lipstick stain may have been fun, the stain is a huge pain! Use baby wipes to clean off this menace. For blood stains, white vinegar and cold water normally work for me. Combat wine stains with club soda. Cool water and liquid dish soap also work. Remove red sauce with white vinegar.

To be honest, I haven't had too much luck removing heavy oil or grease stains, but people have had success treating these stains with baking soda. There are so many recommendations online to help remove various stains. Be sure to visit Clorox.com to research more stain removal remedies. Here's a cheat sheet for quick reference:

COMMON STAINS	REMEDIES THAT WORK
Coffee/tea/latte	White vinegar
Ink	Rubbing alcohol or Hairspray
Lipstick/make up	Baby wipes (Vicky's personal favorite!)
Blood	White vinegar and cold water in equal parts
Red sauce	White vinegar
Wine	Club soda or cool water with clear liquid dish soap
Oil/Grease	Baking soda

Now that we've discussed some great accessories, how to buy them and how to even care for them should a mishap occur, it's also important that you have some fun with your accessories. I know that I certainly do!

Describe ways you have fun with fashion and men's hardwear. What are some items for your hardwear toolkit that you need to purchase or replace?

....

....

....

....

....

....

....

....

....

....

....

....

....

....

....

....

....

....

....

....

....

....

....

....

....

....

....

"To me, clothing is a form of self-expression – there are hints about who you are in what you wear."

Marc Jacobs

MEN'S HARDWEAR

CHAPTER 6 –
BARGAINS

Who wants to pay full price for anything? I certainly don't want to pay full price, ever. Having enough money to pay the full price isn't necessarily the issue. For me, it's the actual thrill of seeking, intentionally looking for and even stumbling onto what I consider a real bargain. This chapter is all about actively searching for that bargain and I'll share some strategies and tips that have helped me over the years. It's still so interesting to me to see how excited I get when I realize just what a bargain, or perceived bargain, something is. It also teaches me patience, as typically the product, service, or other must-have item eventually goes on sale. Plus I think it's great to see how coupons come in handy. I'm not suggesting that everything you will purchase from here on out will be the deal of a lifetime. However, what I am suggesting is that chances are, anything that you will purchase from here on out may be available at a discounted or reduced price. At the end of the day, I've learned that everything is negotiable. YES, everything.

One of my favorite finds (even though the find wasn't for me this particular time), happened around 2009. When visiting my daughter, Danielle, in college at Pepperdine, the family decided to take a day trip and drive down to Cabazon and check out the Desert Hills Premium Outlets. There's something about the word "premium" that draws me in every time. Typically, the premium outlets have higher-end stores and a better selection than that of other outlets. At that time, the Desert

Hills outlets had a Christian Dior store near their Gucci outlet. While in the Dior store, I spotted a beautiful women's beige leather Gaucho saddle bag, complete with the Dior coin and key hardware. Both my daughter and I looked at it and laughed out loud when we saw the steep price tag—it was more than $1,200.

I can still clearly remember having at least a five-minute conversation with Danielle about the price seeing as how we were in an outlet store. I guess for some people, that price really was a discounted price, since the bag retailed for a little over $1,800. Although thinking about how much my wife would love this bag, I just couldn't comprehend the crazy high price tag. As you can guess, the bag remained in the store. Luckily for me, my wife never saw us admiring the bag and never saw the bag. She had her sights set on something else.

A few months later, while we were back home in the DC area, Vicky and I visited a high-end consignment shop in Annandale, VA. As is my custom, I immediately started looking for a real bargain. As I continued to browse around the store, it just so happened that I saw the same Dior bag that Danielle and I had admired months earlier at the Dior outlet. This time, it was hanging on the mannequin in the front window. From a distance, it actually looked brand new. Remember, at that time, the bag retailed for $1,800. The Dior outlet was selling it for $1,200 and this consignment shop listed it at $300. Yes, $300!

It gets better. The bag had the original tags, proving its authenticity, the original duster (protective cloth storage bag designed to keep it clean) and the original Dior store packaging. Bingo! It doesn't get any better than that! I couldn't believe my eyes. I quickly climbed into the display area, grabbed the bag off the mannequin's shoulder and asked the owner to hold it at the register. After Vicky finished looking around, I told her about the incredible deal. To me, it was a no-brainer, so of course I got it for her. Today, almost 10 years later, the bag still goes for no less than $500 on eBay and similar sites. One point that I want to make with this example is that as consumers we get to decide if the price is a bargain based on the value we place on the item in question. For this bag, it was all about the quality of the leather, craftsmanship, details in the stitching, hardware and the uniqueness of the bag itself, and less about the designer or brand.

Incidentally, while our daughter toured the outlets with us in California, she's not a bargain hunter like I am, although she considers herself very thrifty in what very little shopping she does. And, in fact, she doesn't like to shop—at all! I just don't get it. How do you have parents who love to shop and those shopping genes didn't get passed down? Just saying! Perhaps she's scarred from the years of us dragging her from store to store and mall to mall, oftentimes from open to close of business, with a snack or two in between. Interestingly enough, her husband, our amazing son-in-law Dion Watson, loves and I mean loves to shop but only for the real bargains like me! He's a man after my own heart. I've been told he gets his shopping bug from his precious mom, Sophie. I often wonder with a chuckle if they can out shop me! Whenever we visit them out West, we can count on two things—hiking in the mountains and canyons of Malibu and shopping the flea markets for the bargains. Dion's favorite place to shop for one-of-a-kind bargains is The Roadium Open Air Market, located in Torrance, California and open seven days a week. While in town a few months ago, I had the pleasure of riding with Dion to the Roadium. I was in awe of the bargains he found that particular day (I still am!). First was the Alexander McQueen cardigan sweater that retails for more than $475, for which he paid $20 bucks. Next was an All Saints oxford shirt that retails for $100 and cost him $5. Then there was a pair of PRPS jeans that retail for more than $250 and cost him 15 measly dollars and last was Dion's favorite Levi's denim shirt, with a whopping $5 price

MEN'S HARDWEAR

tag at the Roadium. Wow! The bargains are out there!

As you can see, bargain shopping can save you a lot of money on quality, high-end clothes and accessories. However, you have to take the time to look around and find the best price—for you.

I will admit, for far too many years, I didn't have the patience to shop around and proactively go after the best deal. I don't even want to estimate how much money I could have saved had I let patience rule supreme in earlier years. Of course, in life there are things that you just want and think you must have at the moment. In those cases, you may be willing to pay a higher price or full price, but I'm suggesting that that doesn't necessarily have to be the norm. After more than 20 years of intentionally shopping for bargains, I know for a fact that I can get something for less than advertised when I include patience, research, and perseverance in the equation.

So let's talk strategy and tactics. Many department stores price match, offer coupons and have sales. Some even discount their merchandise at clearance centers. Even popular high-end stores have outlets. Consider Neiman Marcus, Nordstrom, Saks Fifth Avenue, Gucci, Prada, Hugo Boss, Giorgio Armani, Ferragamo, Tom Ford, Jimmy Choo, Bloomingdales, and many more stores. The only brand that doesn't have an outlet store anywhere in the world that I know of is Louis Vuitton. My sources tell me that LV burns all defective merchandise, doesn't have outlet stores and doesn't ever discount its products. The only place that I've ever seen a discounted Louis Vuitton item is at a very high-end consignment shop.

In terms of tactics, the first thing I suggest is that you do your homework. The Internet makes it easy to research current prices for almost any item. This is true for cars, electronics, appliances and even fine jewelry, for ourselves and our loved ones!

With the recent birth of my first grandson, I've found great bargains on baby clothes, accessories, and even furniture for the nursery. Bargains are indeed everywhere, you just have to have patience and be willing to spend a little time searching and researching! This also includes price matching. Many stores will honor sales prices from another store if buyers provide them with proof, like showing them their competitor's website or having them call the store directly to confirm. My wife is famous for taking pictures and screenshots to show one store how another store has the same item for less. In every case, the store we're in at that moment, price matches so as not to lose the sale altogether. As you can see, finding a bargain takes some work and effort but I have found that it is absolutely worth it.

My second suggestion is that you check online for coupons. Do this before you go off shopping and while at the store before you make purchase. More recently, Vicky and I were at a high-end store at a nearby premium outlet, looking for a gift for a friend. This particular store normally has their coupons in the store. Store greeters also pass them out as customers enter, thus offering an additional percentage off of the total purchase. Most times, this retailer has same-day coupons offering another 30 percent off either one item or even better, every item purchased. On this particular day, they did not hand any coupons out as we entered, which we found strange. Of course, we instantly asked one of the store associates if there was a coupon. She shared that the current discount pricing was the best price, as some merchandise was already marked down; some by 70 percent off retail and others by up to 50 percent off of outlet prices. Generally, we would have accepted this response and either made the decision to purchase at the stated price or continue to shop around in hopes of finding a better bargain. However, I spotted a beautiful lamb's leather moto style jacket, originally priced at a whopping $1,000 and marked down to just $300! After examining the jacket more closely I was convinced that it would look amazing on Vicky. Although she's not big on leather jackets in general, this one had great detail, functional zippers and was gorgeous; it was a must have in my book. I knew she didn't have anything like this jacket in her closet and one could argue that it was actually a pretty good deal. After convincing my wife that it was a great addition to her wardrobe, she went into gear and started pulling up coupons on her smartphone for the store, looking for an even deeper discount—I admit, we just can't get enough. She politely asked the cashier to try entering coupon barcode numbers from online coupons. She tried multiple coupons—all to no avail. She even found one for their factory and outlet store in Canada—still, nothing. After trying four times with a coupon code that didn't work, the cashier looked through her stack of printed coupons provided by previous customers, gave us a big smile, and scanned one that gave us an additional percentage off the total purchase. The $1,000 buttery soft leather jacket instantly dropped down in price to $200—can you say deal!? I loved this jacket on Vicky so much that if she hadn't gotten it, I had already made up my mind that I was going to get it for her and surprise her later with it. The bottom line is that you must ask, you must be persistent while being extremely cordial to the store employees, and above all else, you must not give up. As previously stated, everything is negotiable.

My third tip has three parts:

1. You have to invest time.

2. Practice patience.

3. Shop around.

Don't be afraid to venture out and plan a few day trips to known stores where you know it will be worth the drive, time, and energy. I am known to travel off the beaten path to find a bargain. It doesn't matter where I am vacationing or visiting, one of the first things I do is look up the locations of nearby or drivable outlet malls, and preferably, premium outlet centers.

The search I undertook to find one of my favorite shoes is a prime example. I had my sights set on a pair of distressed, chocolate-brown, leather crossover, double monk-strapped boots for well over a year. At a hefty price tag exceeding $1,100, I knew I had to let my patience work. No matter how I spun it in my mind, I just couldn't justify spending that much money. I want to reiterate at this point that when it comes to apparel shopping (or buying most anything, for that matter) the question often is not whether you have the money to buy the item the moment you fall in love with it. The question, rather, is how much do you want to pay for it? So, what's the perceived value? Ask yourself if you need the item at the very moment. If not, there is a high probability that you will be able to find it at a discounted price—sometimes significantly reduced—in the future. And the future might be sooner than you think.

My wife happened to be walking through one of my favorite stores after a meeting in New Jersey, more than a year after I first laid eyes on the must-have boots. By now you can probably figure out the rest of the story. Vicky saw the boots on the final clearance sale rack. They just happened to be in my size and they were the last pair in the country—according to the cheeky salesman, at least. That line tends to work on #teamboston quite often. *It's the last pair in the country!* Vicky knew how much I really wanted them and seeing them a year later at a fraction of the cost, she just knew it was meant to be! The price had dropped from more than $1,100 to $275. If you know anything about men's fashion, and especially the price of men's shoes, you know that for a pair of well-made leather shoes that will last a lifetime, this price was a real steal and

MEN'S HARDWEAR

an absolute must-have for me. Needless to say, she snagged the boots and displayed them perfectly, staged on top of the shoe box. When I arrived home from work, I was able to walk in and find the big surprise! This was beyond special and completely unexpected. She teases me to this day about the near permanent grin that I had on my face when I tried on the boots.

As you continue to practice patience, shop off-season. Admittedly, shopping off-season is not always as fun because if you're like me, when you find that incredible bargain, you want to put it on that day and show it off immediately. Why wait? However, when shopping off-season, it is very likely that you will score big by way of deeper discounts, even though you'll be unable to show off your goods right away. I've found that the best time to buy heavy winter coats is in the summer. As with seasonal household items like grills and snow blowers, clothing items like boots, leather jackets or fur coats are typically great steals in the summer months. (Unless you're in an area like Los Angeles where the early mornings and evenings are typically chilly and the middle of the day heats up. In a case like this, you may not see a big sale on leather jackets in August since they can be worn year round.) If you decide to shop off season, be sure to choose wisely by buying classic styles or staple pieces that aren't trendy or time sensitive. Although you may find a great deal, the question remains, will you still love it in six months or even a year later? If you happen to be a frequent traveler, you may find that a sale item that is out of season in your region may be in season at your travel destination. For example, I'm unlikely to need a new pair of swimming trunks in January while in the DC area, but if I head to the Bahamas this winter, they'll be handy.

In addition to off-season shopping, remember not to shy away from second-hand stores and high-end men's or co-ed consignment shops. You may be surprised to see the bargains found when you take the time to visit stores and look around. My absolute favorite consignment stores that have quality men's clothing, shoes, and accessories are on the west coast, by far, and especially in Newport Beach, CA. Even though the great majority of items in these types of stores are second-hand or gently used, I've come across a number of brand new items with the original tags, never worn, yet deeply discounted because of the consignment. Be mindful that sometimes the prices in the high-end consignment stores can be higher than the retail stores and outlets so be sure to compare prices. Now-a-days, with comparative pricing so easily accessible, there's no excuse to ever overpay for anything!

If the consignment route doesn't sound appealing to you, you can still land great bargains online. Websites such as Nordstromrack.com and 6pm.com provide great close-out deals that you may not even find in the brick and mortar outlet stores. Joesjeans.com frequently has close-out deals that offer $200 high-end jeans for $60, with free shipping. You are highly unlikely to beat those types of deep discounts in the big box stores, even with a sale and coupon.

Finally, there's always the option of renting a special or unique piece for a very special occasion. Have you ever considered Theblacktux.com as an option? It's like Renttherunway.com for men. If not, perhaps you may want to check it out. High-end suits and tuxedos that retail for more than $1,200 can be rented for as little as $95. That's not a bad deal at all if you've planned a big night on the town and need to look your absolute best but aren't interested in dropping that kind of cash on an outfit you may never wear again. This is especially true if it's a once-every-five-years type of event, where your weight may fluctuate in between, or if you're attending a once-in-a-lifetime event. I remember several years back my wife had the opportunity to go to the Grammy Awards in Los Angeles. While she looked amazing in the gown she purchased here at home, she would have looked just as amazing and

MEN'S HARDWEAR

saved some money had we been aware of options such as renttherunway.com In fact, I can't remember ever again seeing her wear her Grammy's dress before finally donating it to one of her mentees, who wore it to her junior prom. In addition to donating quality items, you can always re-home new or gently used pieces as a consigner. Most shops will give you 50 percent of your item's selling price.

Something tells me that you've landed some pretty cool bargains too. Take a moment. List some favorite finds, stores and tips that you can share with others.

....

....

....

....

....

....

> *"I am constantly drawing inspiration from everything I see – the places I travel, the people I know and the movies I see."*
>
> *Ralph Lauren*

CHAPTER 7 – FUN WITH FASHION

Who said fashion has to be boring, stiff or dry? I personally believe that fashion is fun and can be fun at any age. In fact, I also believe that fashion can be just as fun for you. Model Patrick Wade suggests we exude confidence in our style of dress. In order to achieve this goal, we must have fun when arranging our wardrobes, and selecting our outfits and their component accessories. Patrick actually practices the art of visualization when doing this. He shared with me that he is so intimately acquainted with his wardrobe—constantly taking inventory, adding and purging as necessary—that in a flash, he can close his eyes and see his entire wardrobe just like that. While I wish I were that much on top of my wardrobe, I am not there yet. When Patrick is out shopping, he envisions what's already in his closet and how the new articles will complement existing clothes.

This is a smart practice for all shoppers. Make sure you know what's in your closet so you don't buy the same thing twice. Buying the same item twice is a sign of having too much in your closet. On the apparel front, taking just a few minutes to peep in and know what you already have will save you in buying the same thing(s) over and over again. In my opinion, there's no fun in that kind of redundancy. I would much rather add to my collection than unintentionally duplicate what's already there. After doing that once or twice (likely even more times), I made a conscious decision to do a better job inventorying the closet to avoid this hassle of dealing with duplicates. Like Patrick, I am really

Tuxedo pants shouldn't be cuffed, and if at all possible, steer clear of the matching tie-cumberbund-pocket square combo that spells r-e-n-t-a-l. They're a huge no-no.) And, if wearing a cumberbund with your fun or traditional black tux, please make sure that the pleats are facing upward and when sporting the tux, money clips are highly recommended versus carrying your standard wallet.

convinced that having loads of fun with fashion is a necessity.

Has fear ever stopped you from trying something new? Certainly, that's happened to me. Or how many times have you gone back and forth with yourself in the mirror, just to talk yourself out of what you initially thought was pretty slick? I quickly learned from those experiences that fashion is personal but doesn't have to be unto death. Here's another example: Who said tuxedos should only be worn in black? In the spirit of fun, I suggest we not limit ourselves to just black tuxedos when formal attire is suggested or required. Remember, tuxedos come in other colors. Consider the dark blue tux modeled by Barrington Little.

There's more than enough room to have total fun with fashion. I have learned that it really is essential that I'm comfortable in my skin and what I put on it. If I concern myself with what others may think about my style, I will go through life wasting precious time. Have an honest conversation with yourself and determine your level of risk. Do you shy away from color? Do you keep everything matching, like your ties and pocket squares? Do you keep plaid away from stripes? No worries, if the answers to some or all of these questions is yes. Just know that there is always time to adjust. However, before the adjustment can be made, take some time to play with different ensembles. Take a walk around the mall and make note of the well-dressed mannequins. Invest in a few quality men's fashion magazines and books as well.

It's funny to me how we sometimes miss out on the fun of fashion by being overly concerned with the opinions of others. People may say, "What in the world is he wearing?!" Don't let that stop you. Such statements typically mean you're inspiring the observer. Your willingness to take risks serves as encouragement for others to try something new. Even high-end designers, such as Gucci and Louis Vuitton, are having fun with fashion. Check out their new prints on classic pieces such as purses, wallets, luggage, and leather goods in general. Look at all of the fun being had by designers such as Ralph Lauren and Lacoste. In recent years they've come out with bright vibrant colors in their entire men's lines, not to mention the oversized pony or gator on their polo style shirts or athletic gear. This is all fun and all a part of reinventing the brand, which is never a bad idea. People tend to have their safe style zones and hold onto time-worn fashion ideas for decades, but there's nothing wrong with looking for creative ways to bring more fun into one's existing style.

What I love about the models featured at the beginning of this chapter, Master Audré Dabney and Master Phelan Harry II, ages ten and eight, respectively, is that at their impressionable ages, they already have a sense of style and how to have fun with it. While they, of course, have the help of their parents in purchasing their clothes and ensuring proper fit, both now know what they do and don't prefer, from a fashion standpoint. Of course, all of this is likely to change as they get older but I find it very cool that they already have fashion sense.

That said, one of the things that troubles me and detracts from the fun that can be had with fashion, is trying to find decent clothes for young boys. Vicky and I often shop for our godsons and now our precious and amazing grandson. Without a doubt, we struggle to find many clothing options for young boys sizes 5 to 10. The struggle is even harder as they mature into youth clothing sizes 12 and up. Even at high-end department stores like Neiman Marcus, Nordstrom, Macy's, Bloomingdales, Saks Fifth Avenue, Ralph Lauren, and the like, (whether online or in the brick and mortar store), the little girls' section is overwhelmingly stacked with beautiful dresses. We have a ball shopping for our goddaughters. (Yes, we have a lot of godchildren!) We truly do struggle to find suits, sports coats, shirts, ties, trousers, and even casual clothes regardless of age or size in the boys section. What are our ten-year-old boys who are tall and in size 8 men's shoes supposed to wear to church, weddings, funerals, and other special events where jeans, sweats and sneakers are inappropriate? Over the years, I would frequently hear the parents of our godchildren complain about this and share their concerns. This caused me to pay more attention to it. Now that I've spent more time shopping for small children in general, I see the huge disparity and totally get their frustrations.

The funny thing is, as I remember it, when I was coming up, my parents were able to find dress clothes for me and my male cousins at stores like Sears and Morton's. However, today it's becoming more and more difficult to outfit our young men. Vicky and I really do empathize with parents of boys, as it appears they have a very limited selection, no matter where they shop. There needs to be more attention paid to this issue to ensure that the fun of shopping and developing one's personal fashion sense doesn't disappear. Now, that wouldn't be a good look. Hey, if you too are having these same struggles, or better yet, have ideas about how to solve them, please send them my way via social media and I'll be certain to share them with other readers of *Men's Hardwear*.

Let's get back to the having fun with our existing closet and/or preparing to have fun with our highly-anticipated enhanced wardrobes. Have you ever considered mixing up what you already have? Chances are that you tend to wear the same dress shoes with the same suit every time that you wear it. After all, it looks good so why chance messing something up? I completely get it, yet I'm challenging you to shake it up a bit and bring some fun into the equation. Let's take that classic black suit for example. Let's say you typically wear it with your favorite pair of double monk-strapped black leather shoes and classic black leather belt. It looks great, you can bank on receiving compliments and it's money in the bank. It works and it works every time. It's highly likely that you'll continue to play it safe with this ensemble because it really does work.

We know the saying, if it's not broke, why fix it?

What I am saying is have some fun with it and take a chance. Try something different. For example, wear the black suit with a pair of deep chocolate, suede, cap-toe shoes and a deep chocolate suede belt and a belt buckle that has a brushed nickel finish. You can tie this all together with a crisp white dress shirt, traditional (brown and black plaid) Burberry cuff links and a fun pocket square to add a pop of color. There's no tie even required for this ensemble. You may be thinking, *Wait a minute, Troy Boston, this is way too much for me all at once.* No problem. How about you try starting by adding fun, colorful socks to your somewhat conservative wardrobe? Before I really got into the beaded bracelets and some other fun accessories, I went crazy with happy socks. At that time, which was many years ago, I only added a few pairs per shopping trip, since they were a little pricey then—as I recall it, $14.00 or higher per pair. While some retailers still sell the happy socks and replicas for well over $12.00 per pair, lately, I've seen them priced as low as $1.40 on Amazon.com and at stores like Marshalls, T.J. Maxx, Last Call, Neiman Marcus, Saks Off 5th, and Nordstrom Rack. This is a risk-free way to ease into the fun.

The bottom line is that regardless of your current style you should take calculated risks when the stakes aren't too high. In so doing, you may find that you're actually having fun as you try new ways to wear and pair your clothes. Plus, you'll have the added bonus of a confidence boost that comes with looking and feeling good in your clothes. When I was Phelan II and Audré's ages (they're pictured at the beginning of this chapter), I do not recall being nearly as fashionable, stylish or creative as they are. However, all of these years later, I can honestly say that I've more than made up for it and I never miss an opportunity to explore, experiment and have fun with my wardrobe now.

Take a moment and journal some new ideas and ways to explore with your existing closet and wardrobe. What items do you typically wear together all of the time? How can you shake it up some? There's no time like the present to break out of that shell. Move away from fear and shyness and just go for it. What do you have to lose?

If all else fails, you can always revert back to your defined basics. Just remember, if you never venture out of your comfort zone, you'll never know how much more fun you could be having with your personally defined style! I encourage you to break out of the conservative shackles that may have been holding you back and unleash the fashion beast within. Why not? Go for it!

....

....

....

....

....

....

....

....

....

MEN'S HARDWEAR

....

....

....

....

....

....

....

....

....

....

> *"Fashion should be a form of escapism, and not a form of imprisonment."*
>
> *Alexander McQueen*

ACKNOWLEDGEMENTS

Special thanks to models, Barrington Little, Robert Murray III, Trevon Barnes, Cliff Johnson, Audré Dabney (Dré), Phelan Harry II (P2), and Patrick Wade for sharing your love and passion for men's fashion! **#Style**

To my Dad, Pernell Boston, and late granddads, Lewis Miles, and Everett Spillman, thank you for teaching me the importance of appearance, character, grooming and the significance of men's fashion at such an early age. Thanks for never compromising. **#Class**

To my father-in-law, Ellsworth Hutchinson Jr., thank you for your consistent example of timeless fashion and how to look, dress and be a gentlemen in any situation. **#Timeless**

Kudos to the incredible parents, Mark and Beatrice Dabney and Phelan and Katresha Harry (PhelanMarc Photography), of the young models (Dre'and P2), for inspiring them and teaching them the importance of fashion while having a sense of style and having fun in the process! **#TrainUpaChild**

To my one and only daughter, my baby girl, Danielle Jai Watson and her best friend and selfless husband, Dion Keith Watson, thank you for the precious and priceless gift of a grandson, Master King Jay Watson, to whom I am able to continue to pass down the traditions and important lessons of timeless fashion—this will be fun! **#TeamWatson**

To my raving fan, best friend, life partner, third-generation writer, author of international best-selling book *3 Slow Nickels*; my hero, inspiration, gym buddy, incredible mother of the best daughter, my soul mate, cheerleader, and wife, Victoria Lynn Boston, I couldn't imagine life without you. Thanks for pushing me to write this book and taking the journey with me. **#BostonStrong**

To Delina Pryce McPhaull, you've done it again! Thanks for partnering with us throughout the entire publishing process. **#Amazing**

To PhelanMarc Photography, because only Team PhelanMarc knows how to capture the essence of every situation with the lens. **#TeamPhelanMarc**

Troy P. Boston

Troy Boston is a senior manager at Washington Gas Light Company, serving the Nation's Capital, Maryland and Virginia. A humble recipient of many corporate and volunteer awards, he has nearly 30 years of faithful and dedicated service to the natural gas supply and utility industry. Troy has always had an eye for fashion and has been a fashion guru his entire life, curating his first wardrobe in high school sewing class and having fun while doing it. He is a passionate mentor and first-class gentleman, helping young men in his local church and community pick their first fitted suits, teaching them how to tie their first neckties and demonstrating the importance of being impeccably dressed, well-groomed and well-mannered.

Married for over 25 years to the love of his life, third-generation writer and author of international best-seller, *3 Slow Nickels*, Victoria L. Boston, Troy and his wife enjoy fashion and thrill in discovering high-end fashions at bargain prices. While this book is focused on men's timeless fashion, Troy has an eye for all fashion that transcends time and space. His attention to detail, innate ability to put together an ensemble at a moment's notice and help others do the same, is invaluable. No matter the season, boys, girls, men and women of all ages frequently seek his advice on fashion for themselves and their loved ones. Both domestically and abroad, Troy can often be found helping struggling shoppers pull an outfit together or advising them as they pick out that something special for a loved one. As a husband, father, grandfather, uncle, leader, and community volunteer, he has helped countless people build and rebuild their wardrobes, as he selflessly offers timeless advice out of his love for fashion. In the next few years, post retirement, he plans to spend his discretionary time working in retail, styling mannequins at high-end designer boutiques, and toying with the idea of opening a "Men's Hardwear" boutique of his own. I would love to keep in touch, so please be sure to keep a close eye out for the next phase of the journey!

Twitter - @Mens_Hardwear   **Facebook** - Men's Hardwear
Instagram - troy.boston   **Email** - tvboston@verizon.net

Made in the USA
Middletown, DE
15 November 2016